To:

From:

Dedication:

FOUR SEASONS OF DREAMS
OTHER SEASONS

THE ORIGAMI OF MY DREAM

Elisa-Nefeli

AN ALBEDO PROJECT PUBLICATION ©
© 2022 ELISA- NEFELI

Unauthorized translation, duplication, photocopying, introduction or distribution partially or fully, under any means, including electronic copying, storage or distribution is a violation of applicable laws. Albedo Project is a trademark and service mark owned by Albedo Project Library all rights reserved. The moral right of Elisa-Nefeli, to be identified as the Author, this work has been asserted in the accordance With the Copyright Designs and Patents Act of 1998All rights reserved. No part of this publication may be reproduced, Stored in a retrieval system, or transmitted in any form or by any means, electronic, mechanical, photocopying, recording, or otherwise, without the prior permission of both the copyright owner and the above publisher of this work. All the characters in this composition are fictitious, and any resemblance to actual persons, living or dead, is purely coincidental.

Acknowledgment

A special acknowledgment to the Amazon Pros team for their help in making this book a reality.

About the Author

Having experienced the hardship of a dictatorship at an early age Elisa-Nefeli decided for a life of action. She advanced in medical studies and the humanities, excelled in different sports and worked in projects relating to arts education self-betterment. She lived across four continents between the West the Far East and Asia. She started writing from an early age. She sees Poetry as painting through words and sharing new vistas.

Important Note

In a literary work, to have the full grasp of its message, it has been observed, that it is important to understand the meaning of the words as used in it. For that, there is a simple Glossary at the end of the book, which defines the words used by the author in a simple way to assist you get a better understanding of the content. This does not replace the utility of a proper Dictionary when available.

Introduction

The Origami of my Dream is the expression of an existence. In my opinion as expressed in this work, the "size" and other preconceived prerequisites to "making it" - do not matter.

The power of expression, the power of creation, can raise one above and beyond that groove of conformity, that batters us around a limited life. That trap, that appears to be the "safe, agreeable way" to go about things – which does not lead however to living and contributing to life for real.

This concept is not about right or wrong. Each one in its own way appears to want to prevail, to have an effect upon life, and prove one self right in his or her choices.

The "Origami of my Dream," considers an existence without such concept. Considers daring, confronting, going for living life above winning or losing – as what matters is to live life not "put it up on a shelf to be looked at and "admired."

It does not matter if others know or not know what you had to go through – to live such life. What matters is what you contributed to life and the living. It could be my, re-definition of essential success, of personal integrity toward one's dreams.

It is the performed action, contribution, no matter how small, no matter the odds that matters and pushes one forward in the most essential way. Instead of wanting to take from life and others it is the concept of experiencing, contributing, co-existing with no concern of "getting," winning or losing.

This is true richness; this is true value for me, and a worthwhile interaction with living. No matter the dangers, social exclusion, and odds, that such life may bring about.

Every one can make a difference, every one has a value, in his or her way and own nature. Our nature that is not "animal" or "material". Our contribution is in bringing life to things, a certain quality to it, not the use of force to overcome life. Yes the universe is vast and the odds are great but life is a game after all.

"The Origami of my Dreams" stands for that power to live and dream. To re-store to re-create, to persist despite of size, form, limits, or character.

I wish you be yourself and you take on this adventure to express and help make a better world making any "Origami" frail looking dream a steady and unshakable reality.

Elisa-Nefeli

"To all dreamers of a better tomorrow
to all doers that help bring about a better tomorrow."

THE ORIGAMI OF MY DREAM

Upon the lips

of a dream

red lipstick

the sunset spread

It then revolved

and stared at me

in gold

With its orange colour

the hour ticked

A fluff I collected

of white cloud

and a fountain pen

filled with water falls

to mark my being

within this moment

In a timeless bit

I cast

fold by fold

a structure

an Origami

made of east

made of colour

A tiny paper boat

small and vivid

to sail me

peacefully

on those

smiley lips

of fancy

Upon the blue

of a sea

I carefully delivered it

to drift on it gently

On its bridge

I wrote

"Have a good trip"

and "May God provide"

Upon its stern

I painted

a little mermaid

As the ship

distanced

with a delicate bob

I saw her

looking ahead

proud and strong

Her tail curled

her chest straight

her hair a crest

of salt and satin

As she sailed

I saw her

calling for laud

at the seagulls

They rose white

as they flew past

they chanted her

sealing her beauty

in a seagull psalm

I let it go

free

upon a picture

of an immense

turquoise

I let it sail

with direction

the unknown

with compass

my tomorrow

Small fragile

but also great

like a future

I grew through it

perceiving

I felt it

as it sailed

how it bobs lightly

toward deep waters

toward

that unknown indigo

small but dauntless

like this composite

existence

It sailed stably

it weaved

slowly

calmly

stern and certain

to the immensity

ahead

But even if small

I saw it standing

knightly

resolute

Great like a virtue

that pulses comfort

Crimson like an intention

Bright and elegant

like a Japanese gift

In its delicate motion

it spelled

the "Ds" of dreams

within me

Light

like a Zephyr

in an afternoon

that caresses you

imperceptibly

and salty

as it passes

With its

card mariner

who pull up

a vellum sail

that spreads fearless

under the azure

sight of a sky

On its stern

tends and holds

some golden rays

to reach life with a sun

to wave creation

with a game

till triumph

till peace

And it sails on

bobbing

and dashing

here and there

to see it all

to live it all

It's sail

full of wind

climbing or descending

in a straight forward

direction

Having cheerful

sun rays

for passengers

that shine and laugh

like children

like understandings

Pull the sheet

anchors

hang upon the sky

a paper moon

with life for Captain

with compass

intention and mind

With waves for moments

Sail through

discovering new lands

in the mundane

or mythical alike

To mark that fantasy

with the smile of

every while

that sails by

While at sunset

through orange

the hour gazes

Wind

carries me

upon this paper ship

while the hour

invisibly

tends crimson

and gold

aspirations

That hour that tends

a whisper

full of value

that sways

the rhythm of living

a pattern

a marked direction

a life

upon that small

Origami ship

www.ingramcontent.com/pod-product-compliance
Lightning Source LLC
Chambersburg PA
CBHW071128130526
44590CB00056B/2992